Christ Over Cancer Coloring Book

© 2018 Ruby Winters

All Rights Reserved.

This book or parts thereof may not be reproduced in any form, stored in any retrieval system, or transmitted in any form by any means—electronic, mechanical, photocopy, recording, or otherwise—without prior written permission of the Publisher

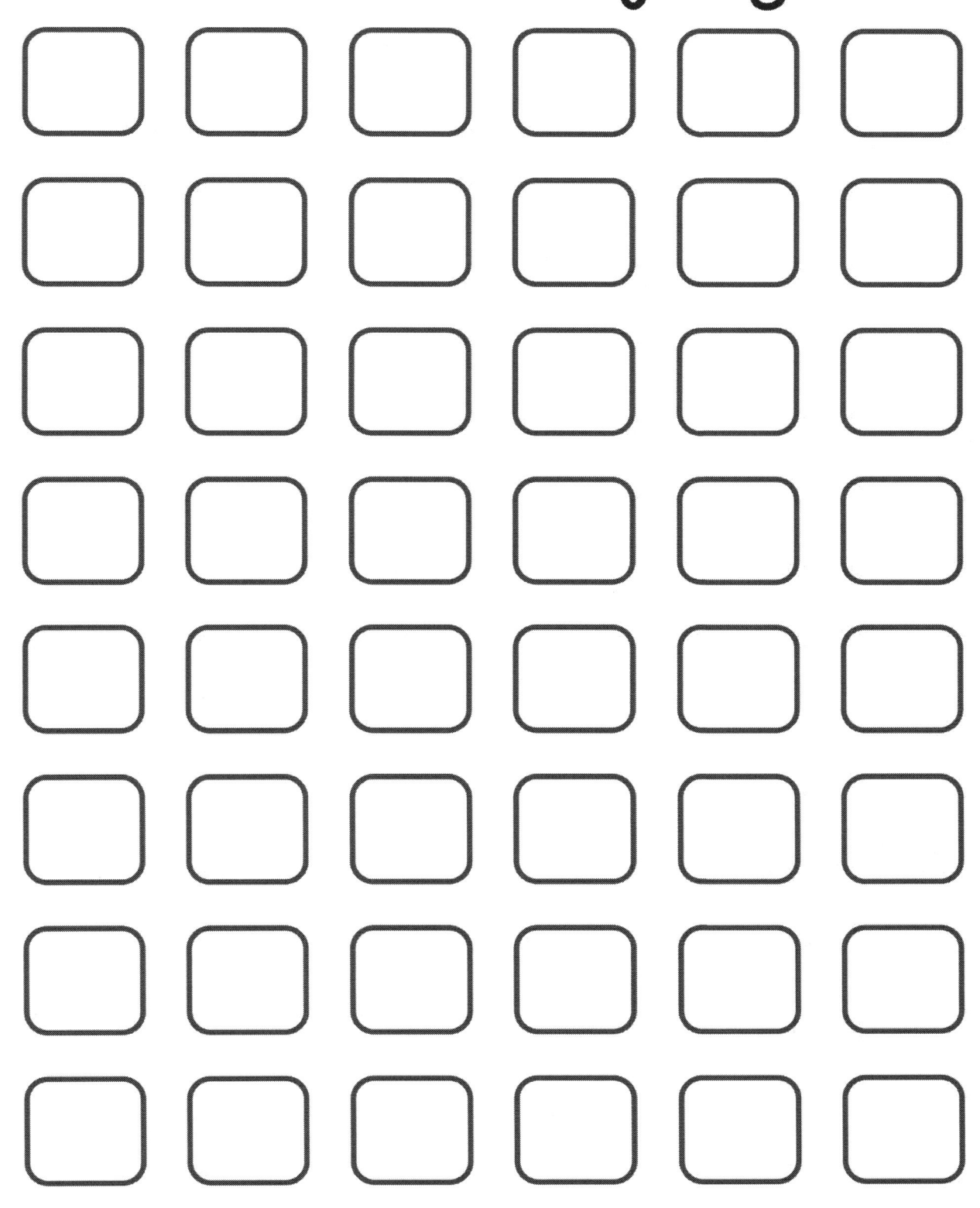

Color Test Page

Color Test Page

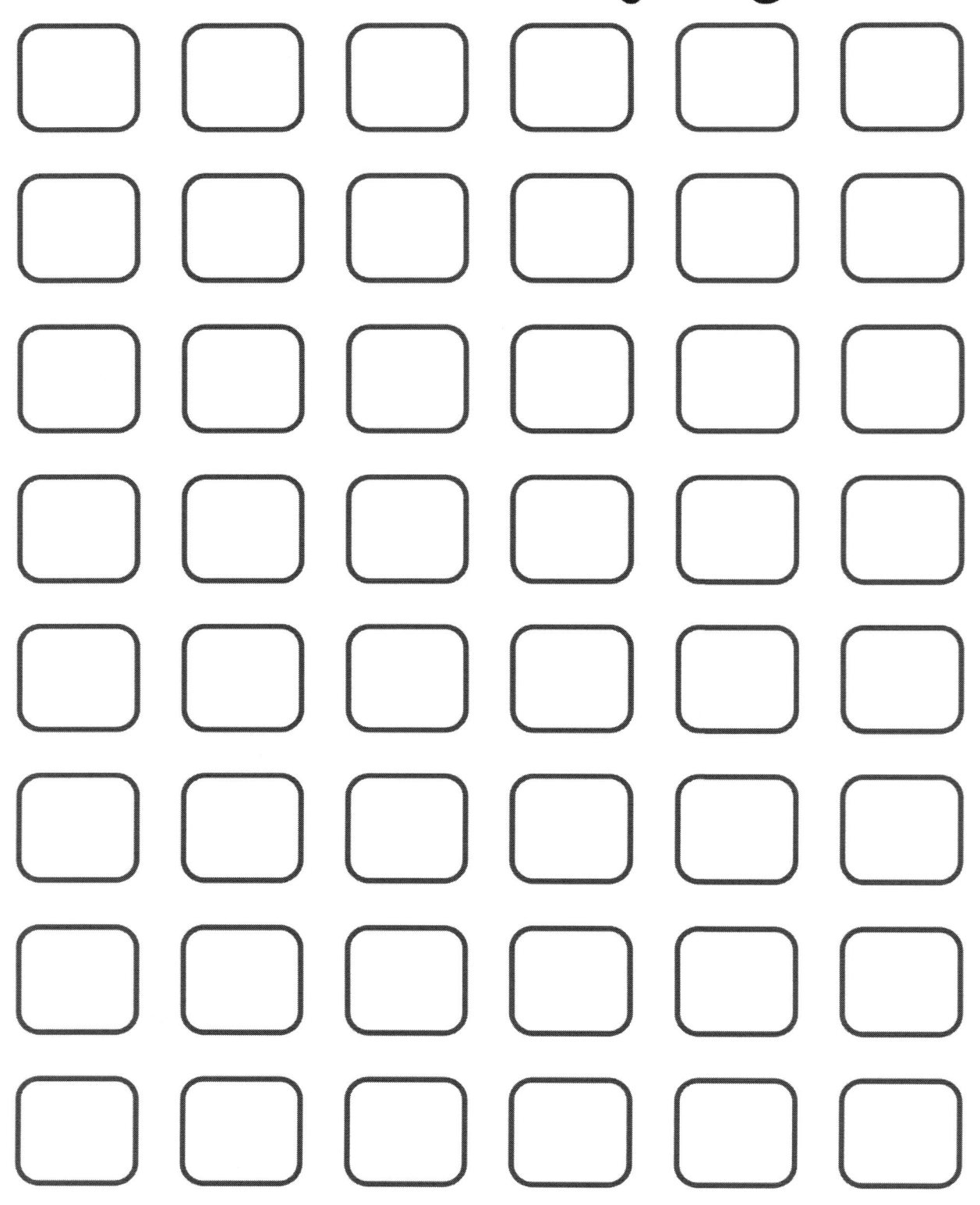

Love never gives up one

1 Corinthians 13

THE JOY OF THE LORD IS YOUR STRENGTH

NEHEMIAH 8:10

So do not fear, for I am with you; do not be dismayed, for I am your God. I will strengthen you and help you; I will uphold you with my righteous right hand.

Isaiah 41:10

The Lord will fight for you; you need only to be still.

Exodus 14:14

The tongue has the power of life and death, and those who love it will eat its fruit.

Proverbs 18:21

Be strong and courageous.

Do not fear or be in dread of them,

for it is the Lord your God who goes with you.

He will not leave you or forsake you.

Deuteronomy 31:6

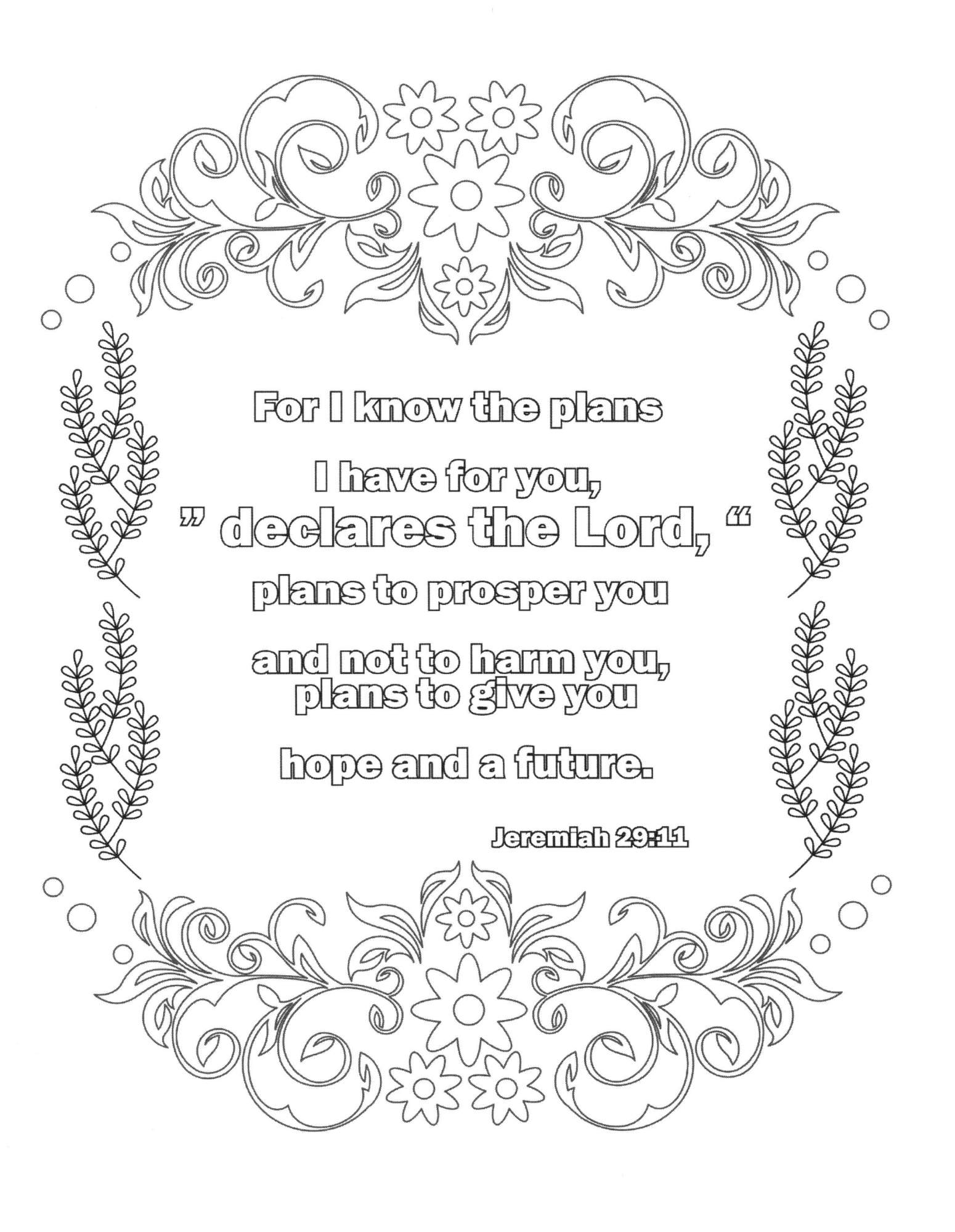

For I know the plans I have for you," declares the Lord, " plans to prosper you and not to harm you, plans to give you hope and a future.

Jeremiah 29:11

But for you who revere my name, the sun of righteousness will rise with healing in its rays. And you will go out and frolic like well-fed calves.

Malachi 4:2

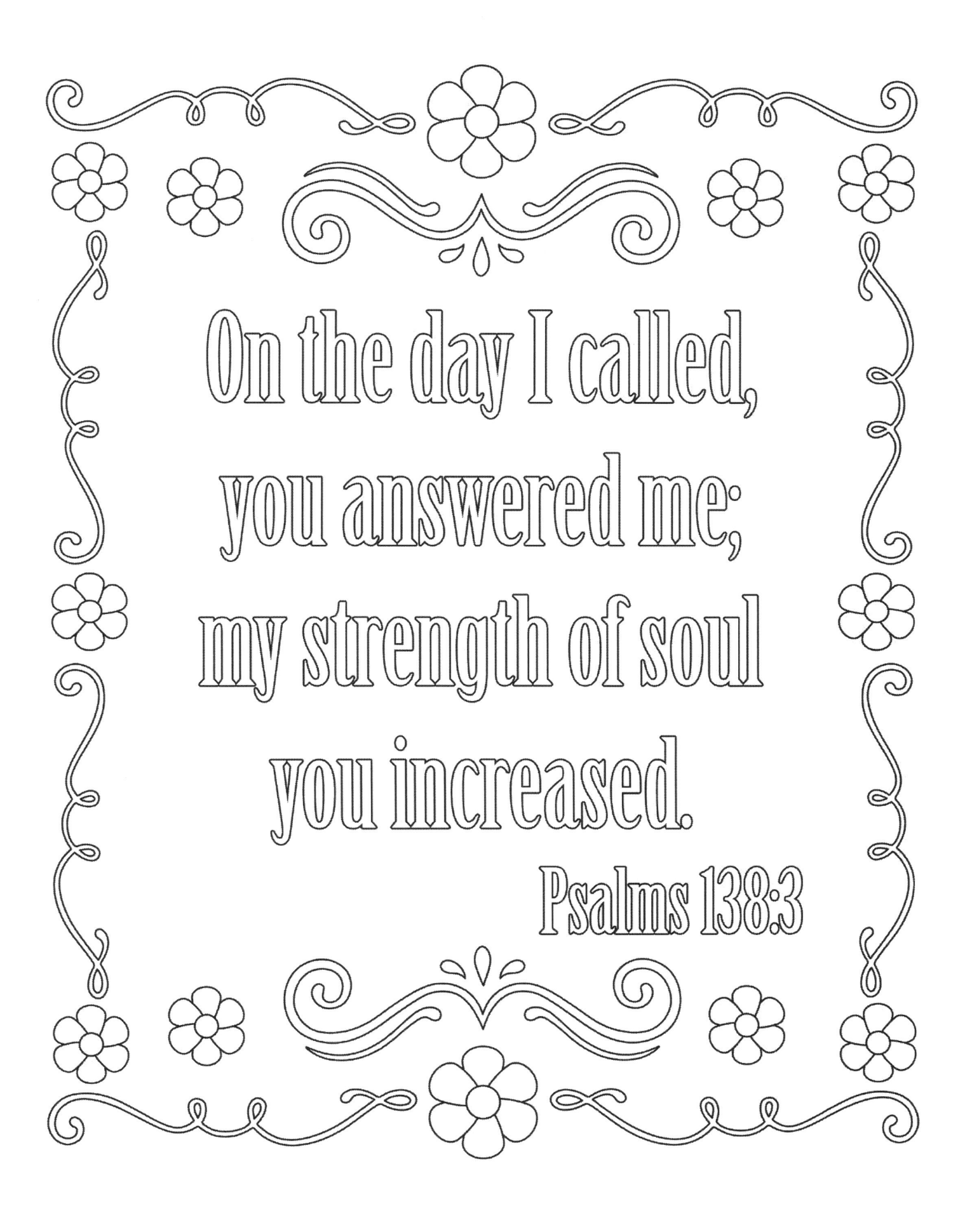

On the day I called,
you answered me;
my strength of soul
you increased.
Psalms 138:3

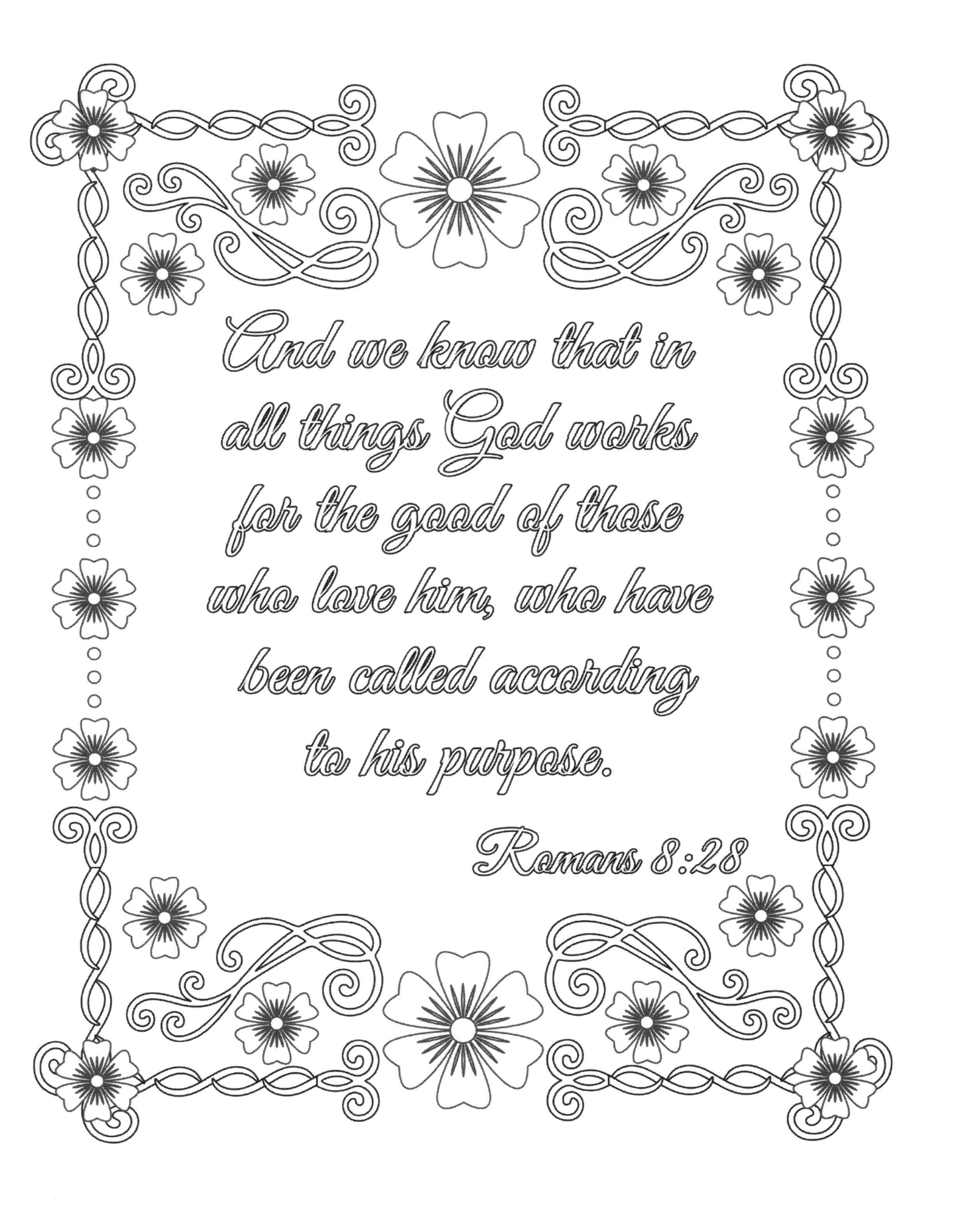

And we know that in all things God works for the good of those who love him, who have been called according to his purpose.

Romans 8:28

Fear the Lord, you his holy people, for those who fear him lack nothing.

Psalms 34:9

Now faith is confidence in what we hope for and assurance about what we do not see.

Hebrews 11:1

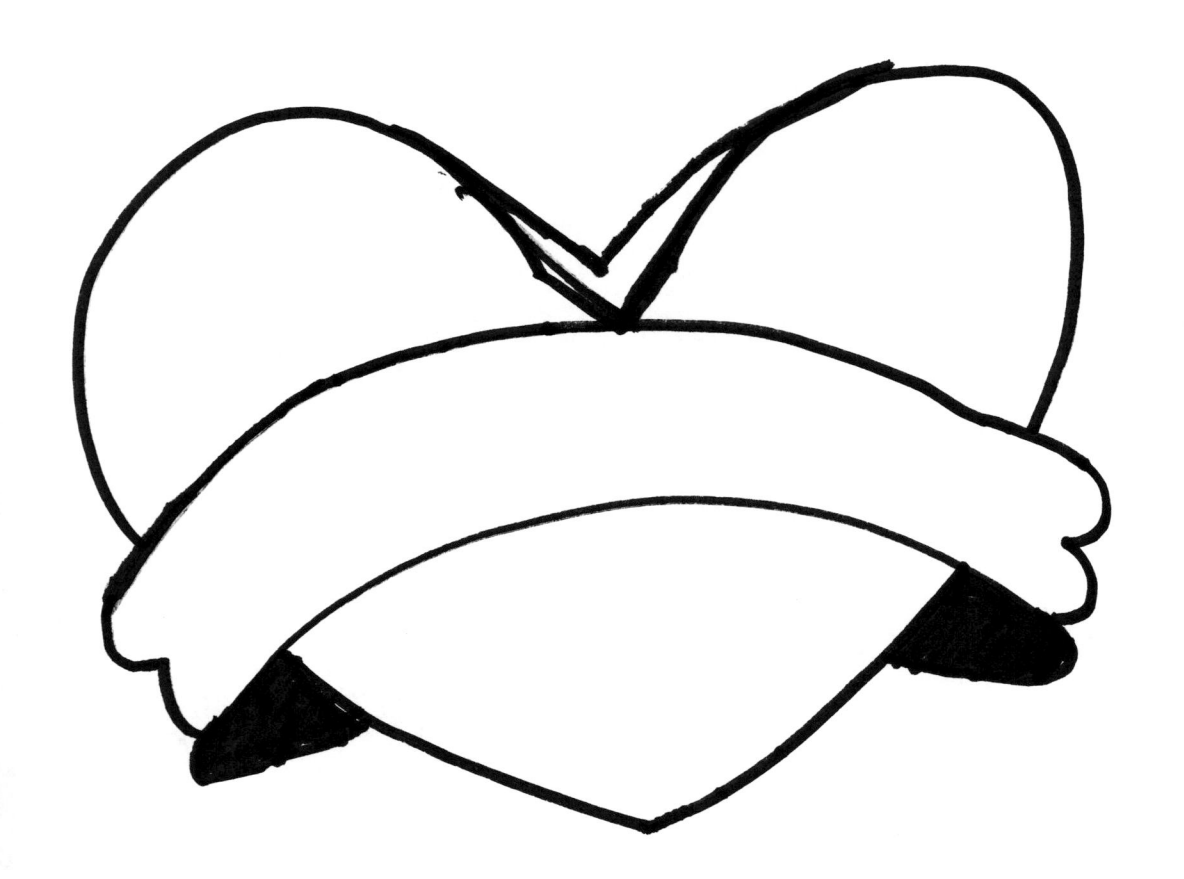

Because you know that the testing of your faith produces perseverance.

James 1:3

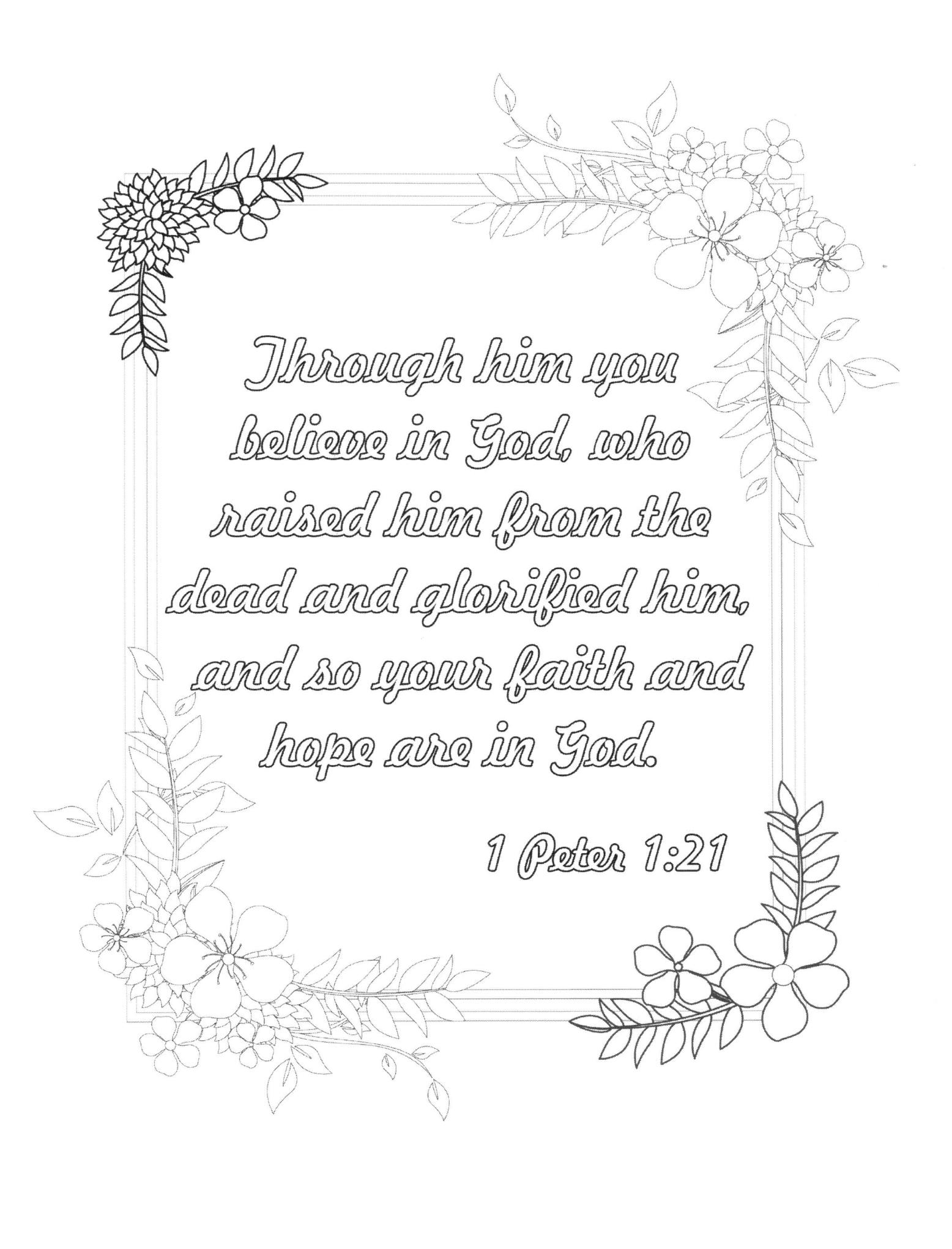

Through him you believe in God, who raised him from the dead and glorified him, and so your faith and hope are in God.

1 Peter 1:21

So then, those who suffer according to God's will should commit themselves to their faithful Creator and continue to do good.

1 Peter 4:19

Consequently, faith comes from hearing the message, and the message is heard through the word about Christ.

Romans 10:17

He send
out his word and healed them;

he rescued them from the grave.

Psalm 107:20

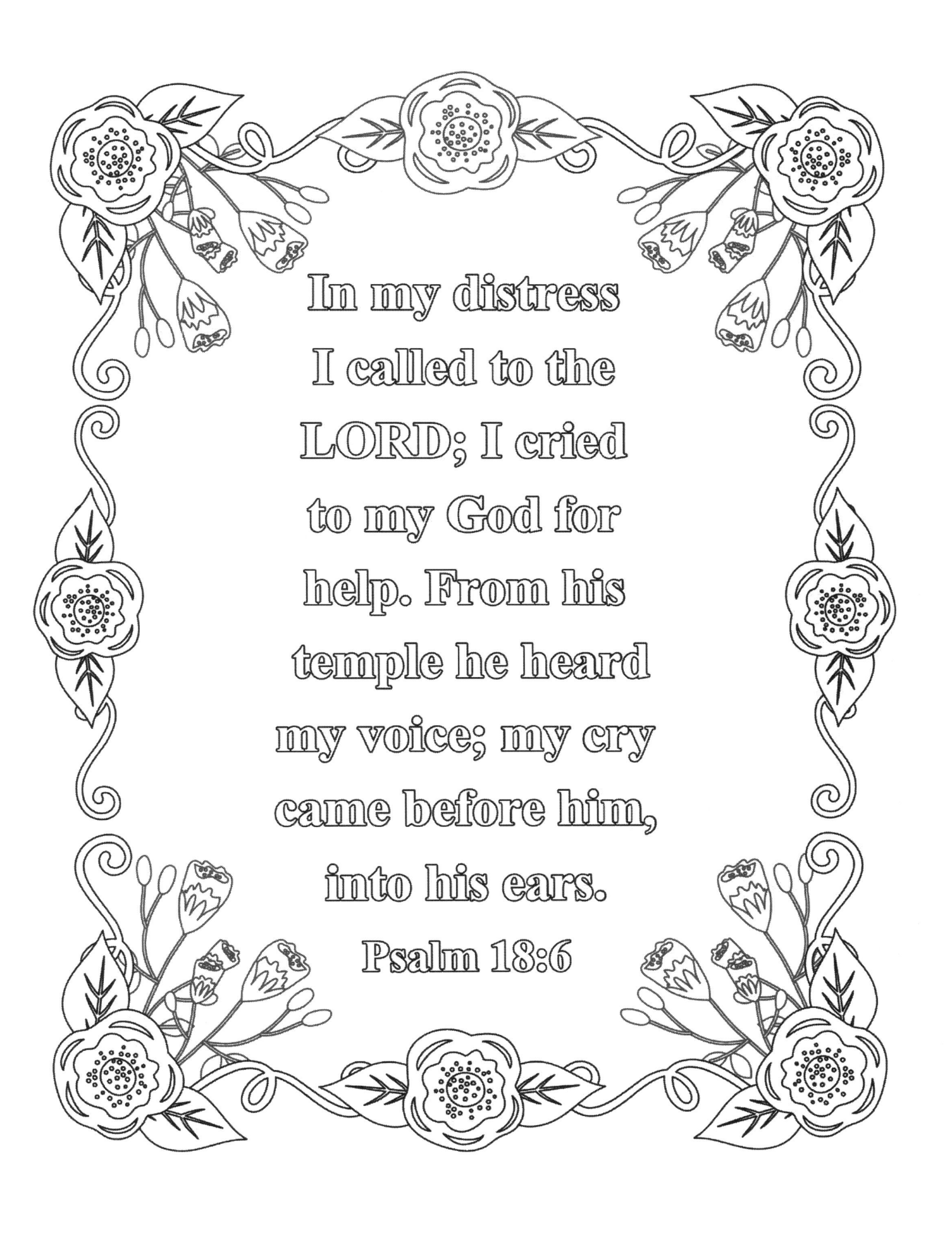

In my distress I called to the LORD; I cried to my God for help. From his temple he heard my voice; my cry came before him, into his ears.

Psalm 18:6

There is a time for everything, and a season for every activity under the heavens.

Ecclesiastes 3:1

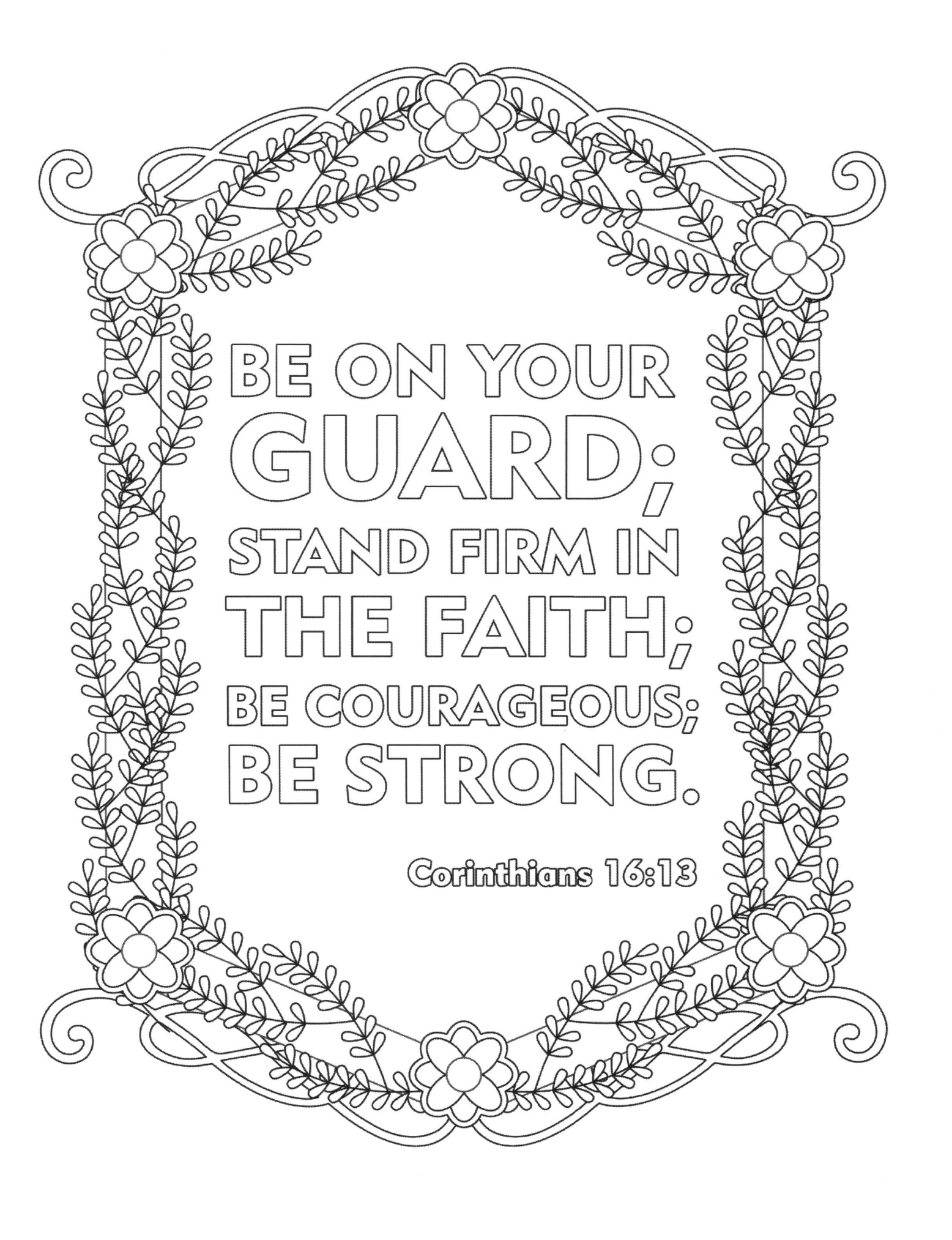

BE ON YOUR GUARD; STAND FIRM IN THE FAITH; BE COURAGEOUS; BE STRONG.

Corinthians 16:13

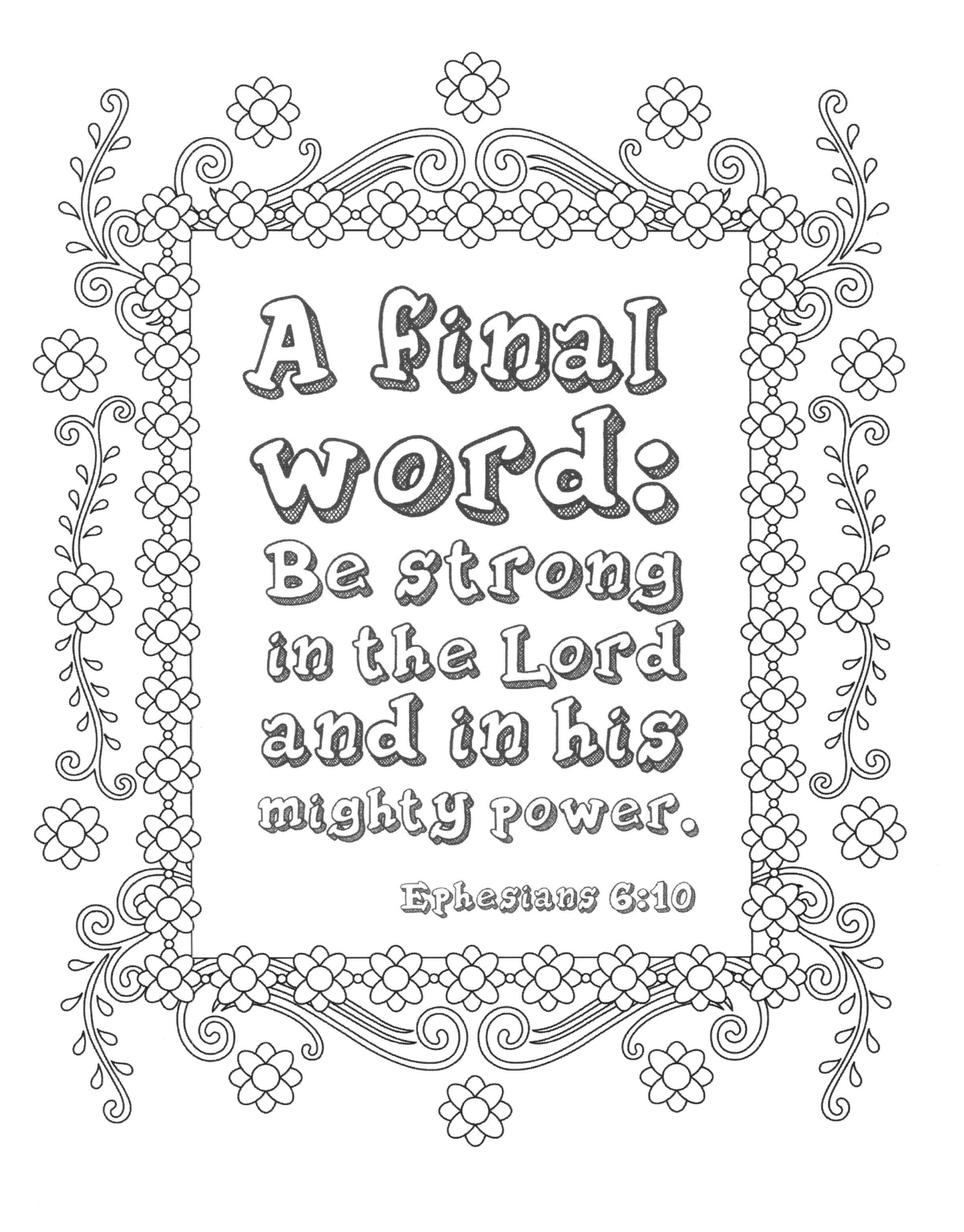

A final word: Be strong in the Lord and in his mighty power.

Ephesians 6:10

For the LORD is good and his love endures forever; his faithfulness continues through all generations.

Psalm 100:5

I can do all things through Christ who strengthens me.

Philippians 4:13

The LORD is a stronghold for the oppressed, a stronghold in times of trouble.

Psalm 9:9

The LORD is good, a strong refuge when trouble comes.

He is close to those who trust in him.

Nahum 1:7

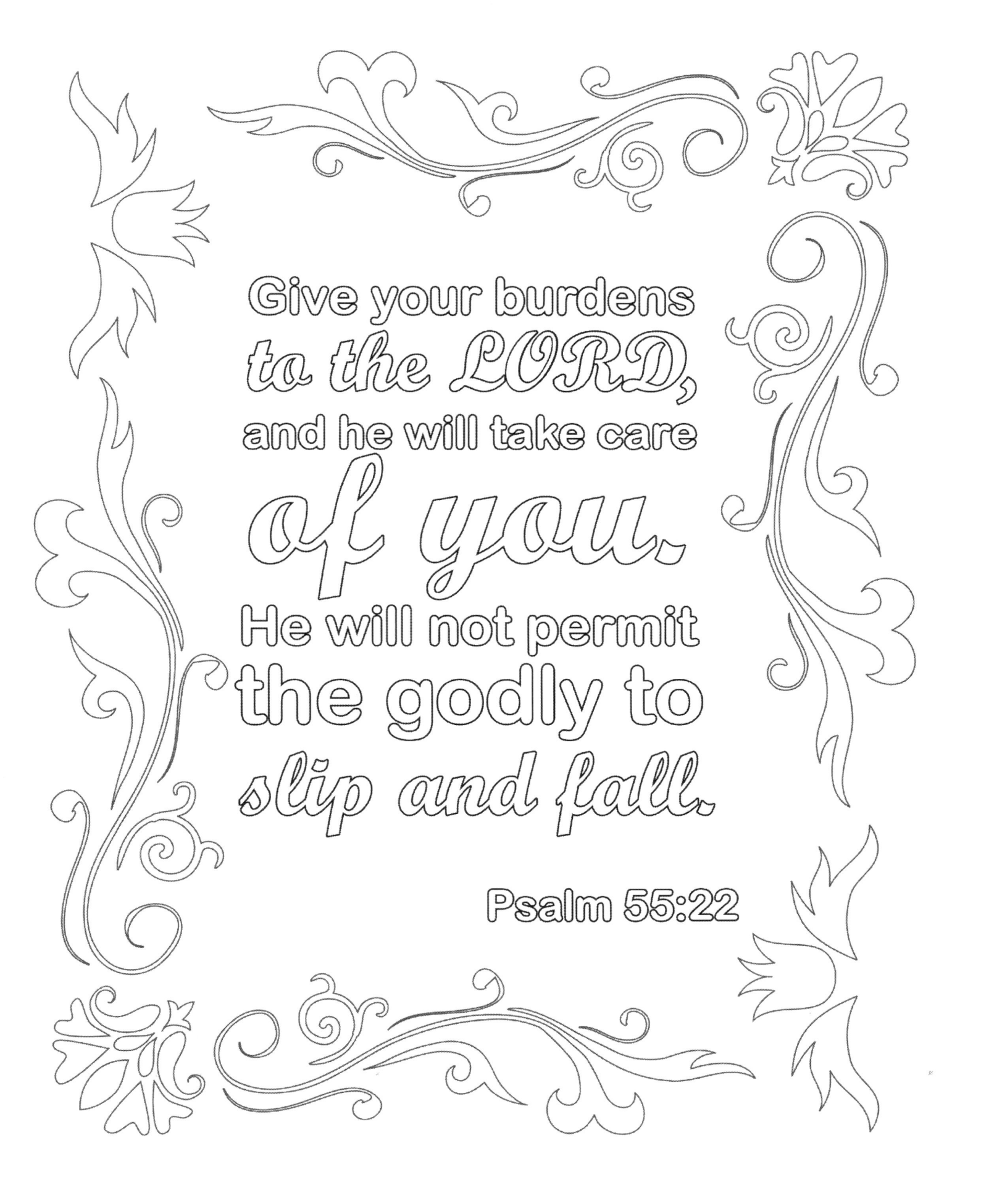

Give your burdens *to the LORD,* and he will take care *of you.* He will not permit the godly to *slip and fall.*

Psalm 55:22

In my distress I called to the LORD, and he answered me.

Psalm 120:1

Then call on me when
you are in trouble,
and I will rescue you,
and you will give me glory.

Psalm 50:15

For the LORD will

not reject his people;

he will never for

sake his inheritance.

Psalm 94:14

Those who know your name trust in you, for you, Lord, have never forsaken those who seek you.

Psalm 9:10

For everything there is a season, and a time for every matter under heaven.

Psalm 94:14

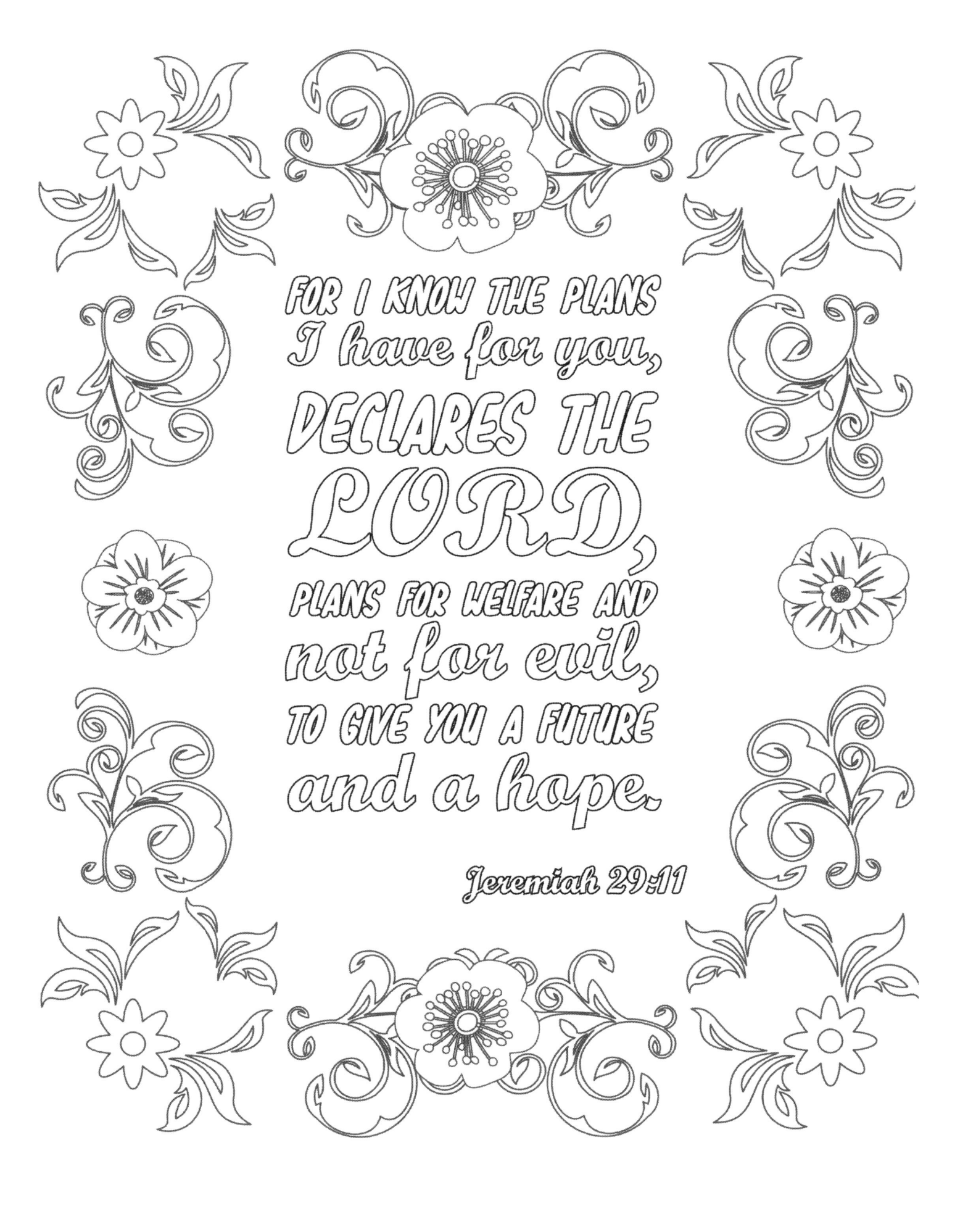

For I know the plans I have for you, declares the LORD, plans for welfare and not for evil, to give you a future and a hope.

Jeremiah 29:11

The Lord sustains him on his sickbed; in his illness you restore him to full health.

Psalm 41:3

When you go through deep waters, I will be with you

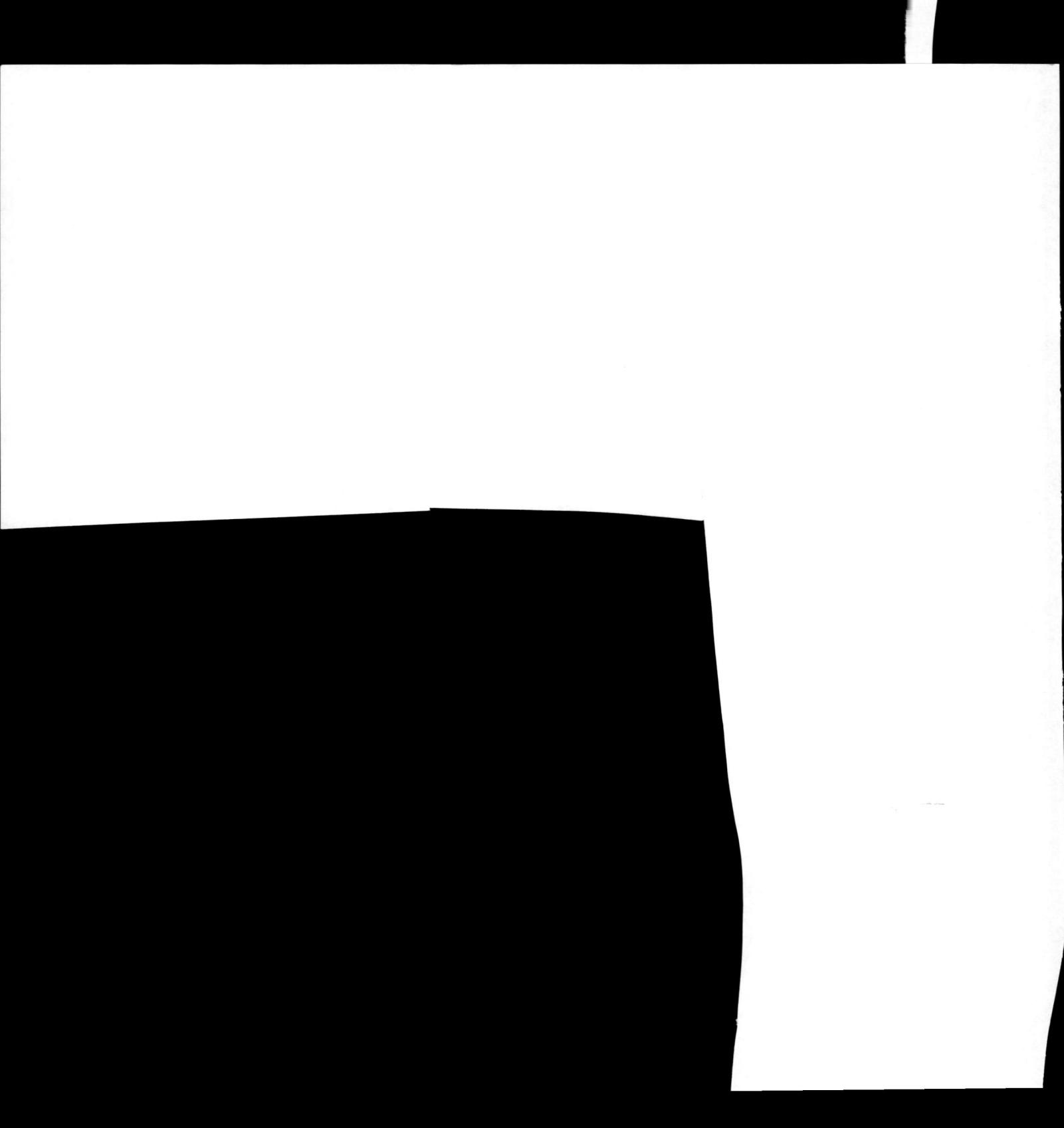

Cast your cares upon the Lord, He will sustain you; He will never permit the righteous to be moved.

Psalm 55:22

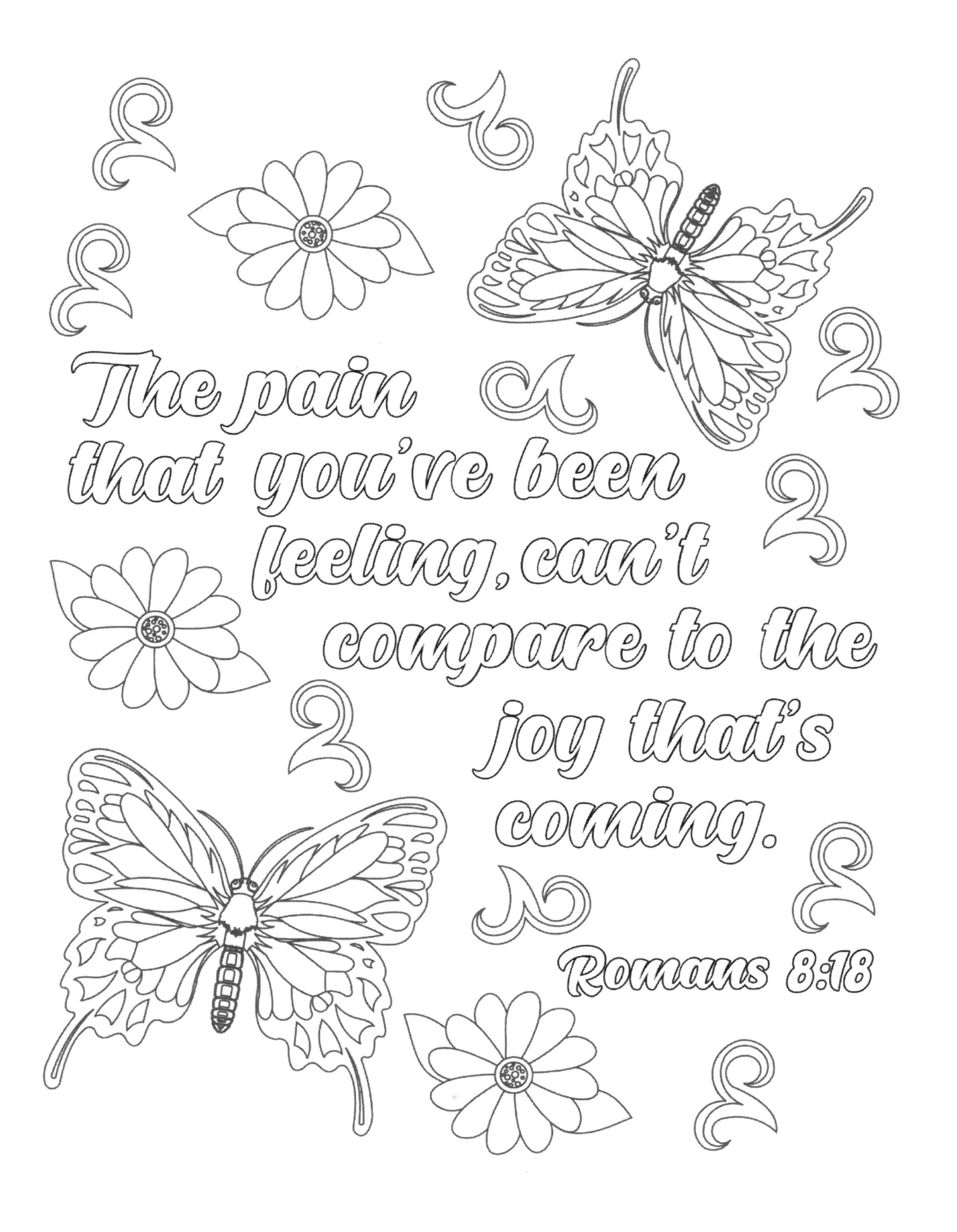

The pain that you've been feeling, can't compare to the joy that's coming.

Romans 8:18

And I am sure of this, that he who began a good work in you will bring it to completion at the day of Jesus Christ.

Philippians 1:6

Be strong AND COURAGEOUS. IT IS THE LORD your God who goes with you. He will not LEAVE YOU OR forsake you.

DEUTERONOMY 31:6

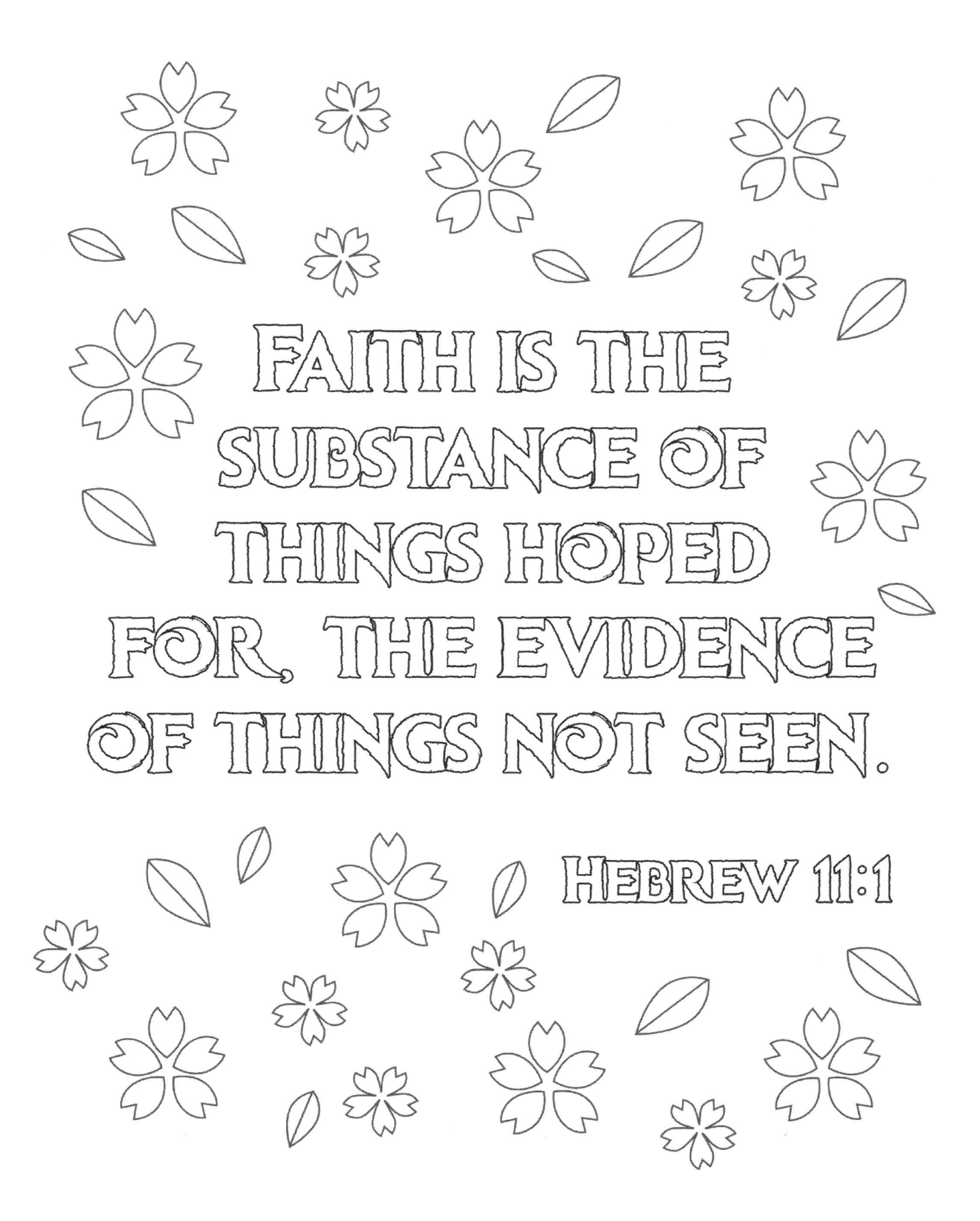

Faith is the substance of things hoped for, the evidence of things not seen.

Hebrew 11:1

And the prayer of faith shall save the sick, and the Lord shall raise him up; and if he has sinned, he will be forgiven.

James 5:15

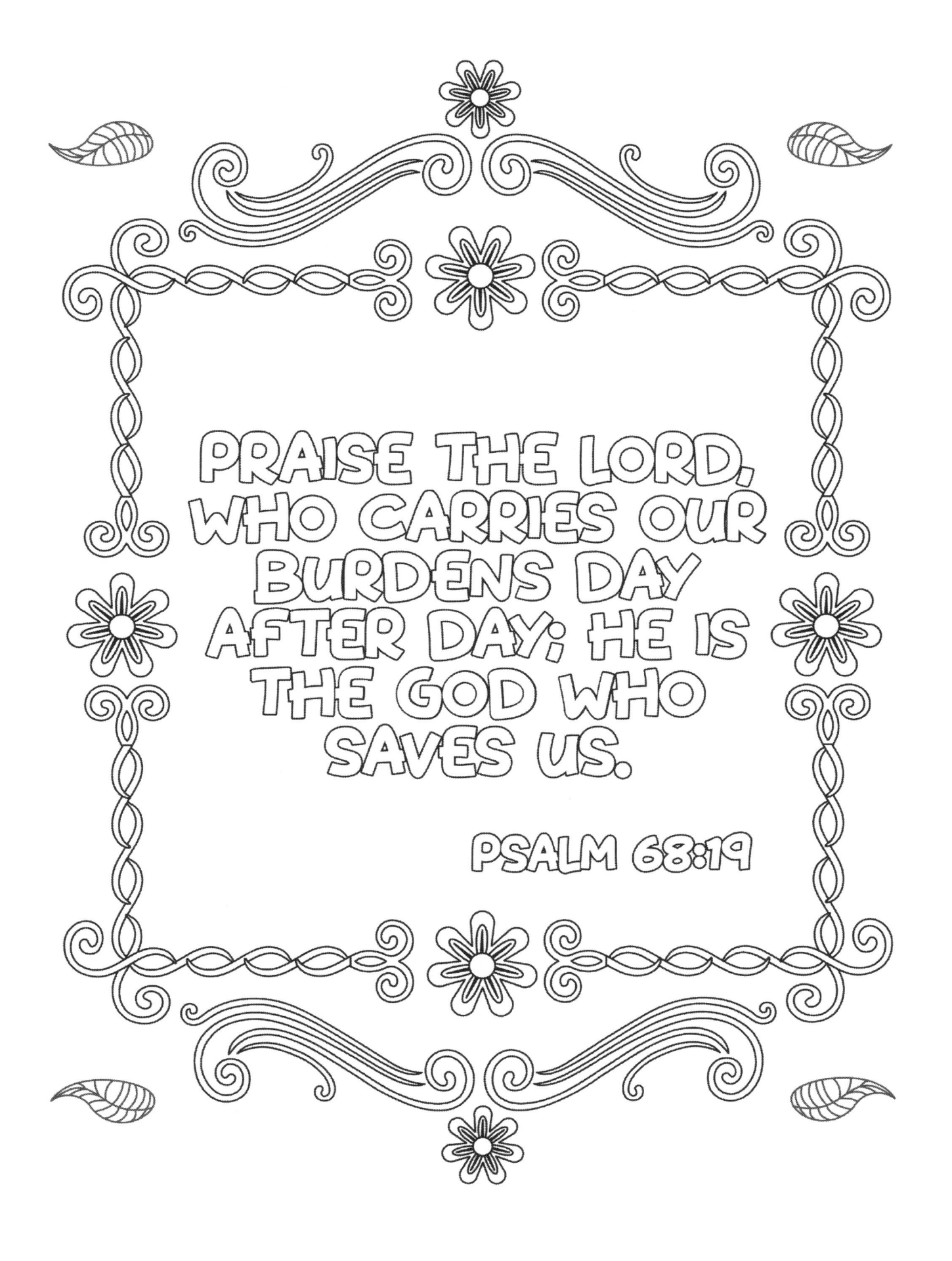

Praise the Lord, who carries our burdens day after day; he is the God who saves us.

Psalm 68:19

You answered me when I called to you; with your strength you strengthened me.

Psalm 138:3

God is our shelter and strength, always ready to help in times of trouble.

Psalm 46:1

The earnest prayer of a righteous person has great power and produces wonderful results.

James 5:16

A tranquil heart is life to the body, but passion is rottenness to the bones.

Proverbs 14:30

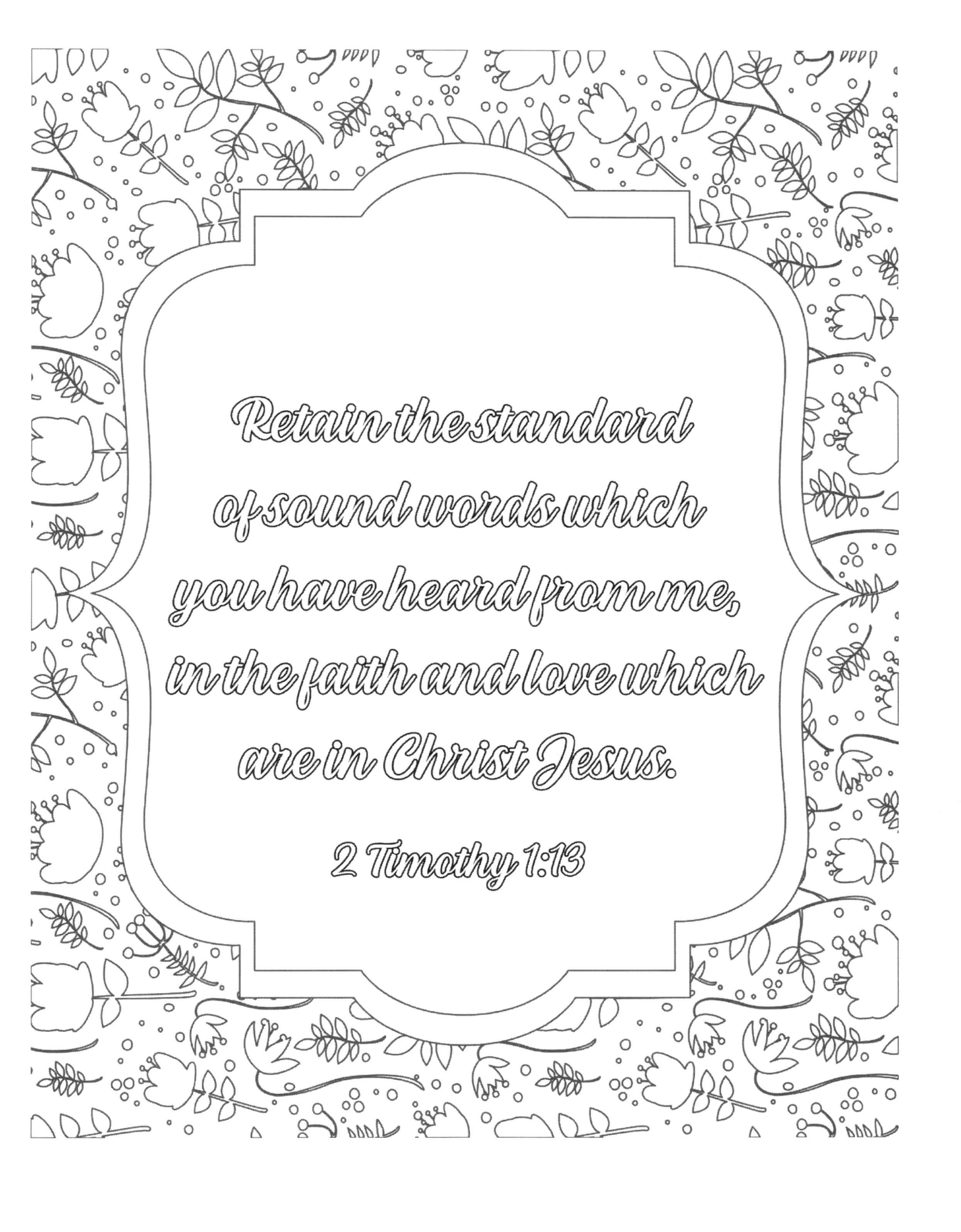

Retain the standard of sound words which you have heard from me, in the faith and love which are in Christ Jesus.

2 Timothy 1:13

But the Lord Stood With Me & Gave Me Strength

2 Timothy 4:17

Thanks for purchasing and coloring this activity book!

Do you want to know a secret? Amazon and Etsy reviews are *super important*. Without them, independent artists like us are dead in the water. When we publish our books on Amazon and Etsy, reviews are crucial for getting colorists to try out our new material because we don't have a major publishing company to help us. Instead, we have amazing colorists who support us like you ☺ It's easy to love our books after trying them, but for first-time customers, it depends on reviews.

Leaving a review is easy and only take a few minutes. Simply rate the book on a scale of 1-5 stars and share your thoughts, what you loved most, or what you'd like to see in the future.

It is **thanks to wondering folks like you** who support independent creators like us that allow us to keep making more awesome stuff and build an amazing community. We can't wait to launch our next great coloring book – maybe it'll be one of your suggestions!

Thanks for all your support,
Ruby at Kingsley Publishing

WANT MORE FUN STUFF?

Join our email list here for **a free printable coloring book,** tons of freebies, giveaways, flash sale alerts and more fun!

http://bit.ly/GetFreeColoringBook

Want some printable fun or want to request something custom made just for you? Visit us on **Etsy**:

Etsy.com/shop/KingsleyPublishing

Join the community and share your art on **Facebook**.
Facebook.com/KingsleyPublishing

Made in the USA
San Bernardino, CA
09 August 2019